Last Greetings from

ST. KILDA

by

BOB CHARNLEY

Hebridean Heritage Series

St. Kilda Pier, from the Land.

'St. Kilda Pier', along with Derby, Newcastle, Northampton, Southport and Ayr, is in Australia. It is possible to count in excess of three hundred and fifty people on this postcard, a crowd far greater than the population of St. Kilda, Scotland at any time in history.

INTRODUCTION

This book contains a selection of pre-evacuation picture postcards of St. Kilda taken from my own collection of between five and six thousand Hebridean postcards and photographs.

Fellow collectors of Scottish postcards already know how difficult it is, almost sixty years after the evacuation, to find cards of St. Kilda and especially to locate postcards posted from the island during the thirty years that it had a Post Office. My good fortune is that I found the majority of my items at a time when prices were reasonable. Those days have almost gone and if you could find every card illustrated in this book they would cost many hundreds of pounds today.

For all those who have worked on, or visited, St. Kilda I hope this selection of early postcards will prove enjoyable. It is not my intention that this should be a book about the island (there are very many books available in both new and second-hand bookshops) but to introduce St. Kilda to fellow enthusiasts who have no concept of how the island looked at the beginning of this century or what happened on the island itself. With this in mind, I will dedicate this book to an anonymous postcard dealer from Hampshire who, in 1988, had a postcard of 'St. Kilda' in their stock priced at £2.50. I purchased the card and it is reproduced opposite. Perhaps it will help the Publisher capture some sales in Australia.

Bob Charnley, August 1989

St. Kilda, from Dun

The St. Kilda group is located fifty five miles due West of Tarbert, Isle of Harris and over 110 miles from the Scottish mainland. The main islands are Dun, Soay, Boreray and Hirta. Most references to St. Kilda actually refer to Hirta, the largest island in the group.

These four postcards show something of the scenery of the islands and stacks which together form the group known as St. Kilda.

Island and Hill of Oshival in the West Coast, St. Kilda.

St. Kilda and Stack Lee

Borrera and one of the great Gannet Stacks, St. Kilda.   Copyright.

A large number of Edwardian picture postcards of St. Kilda bear the caption "Natives of St. Kilda", and it would be fair to say that the great majority of the summer tourists came to stare, poke around, and photograph these 'Natives'.

This voyeuristic attitude seems rather degrading from today's standpoint, but was encouraged at the time by both the press and the shipping companies. Indeed, the latter used it as a selling point of their cruises and implied that the traveller would see something unique. The right-hand card shows some of the tourists visiting the island and meeting the St. Kildan children.

Taken during the filming of 'St. Kilda; Britain's Loneliest Isle' this 1923 view shows Mae MacDonald (the girl in the floral and striped pattern dress) with some of the other St. Kildans.

Natives of St. Kilda   Valentine's Series

Photographed in 1890, six of the natives sit at the entrance to the store house and church. In an attempt to maximise use of the photographs, Valentines super-imposed these figures onto other Highland landscapes and sold them all over the Highlands and beyond.

MacBraynes is the most familiar name for tourists to the Inner and Outer Hebrides today, but for those visiting St. Kilda in the first decades of this century, the choice was between John McCallum & Co. of 87, Union Street, Glasgow (the S.S. "Hebrides") and Martin Orme & Co. of 20, Robertson Street, Glasgow (the S.S. "Dunara Castle").

Before the Great War, the S.S. "Hebrides" sailed to St. Kilda on pre-announced dates at a cost of £10 per person. A 1906 postcard posted from St. Kilda in July that year by a Mr. Gibson chronicles the outward journey as follows:

"Monday 6.25 pm depart Greenock S.S. "Hebrides".
Tuesday 4.00 am at Port Askaig, Islay; 7.00 am arrive Colonsay; 11.30 am at Oban; 3.45 pm at Tobermory, Mull; 7.00 pm at Coll; 8.30 pm at Tiree.
Wednesday 2.00 am depart Tiree; 8.00 am at Rhum; 10.00 am at Soay; Carbost; Colbost, Skye; arrive 3.00 pm Dunvegan, Skye; 3.45 pm depart for Lochmaddy.
Thursday 2.00 am arrive at St. Kilda."

Martin Orme's brochure for the S.S. "Dunara Castle" was similar to that of the "Hebrides" although the description was more florid. The 'Prefatory' offers "... no more pleasanter trip ... among those lonely salubrious Isles, around which blow the vitalising breezes from the Atlantic. Glimpses are to be had of the primitive ways of life that are vanishing. Since the remotest of times a halo of romance has lain around the Isles ..."

In 1929, the two rival companies merged to create McCallum, Orme & Co. Ltd., and on New Years Day, 1948, the company was absorbed by David MacBrayne Ltd., better known today as Caledonian MacBrayne.

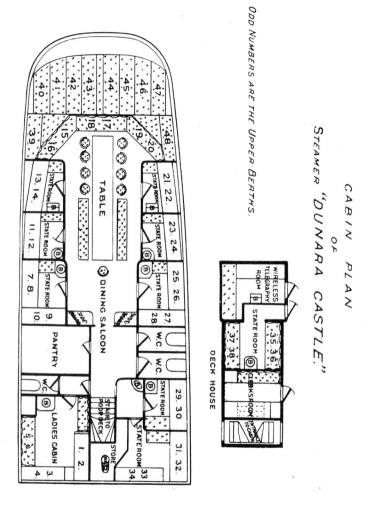

St. Kilda. The Bay

Valentines Series

A postcard by Valentines issued in 1905, using an 1890 photograph. The "Dunara Castle" is in the bay while some of the crew have just landed on the island of Hirta. Stores and tourists alike, all came ashore from these small boats.

S.S. "Dunara Castle"

Built in Port Glasgow at Blackwood & Gordon's yard, the "Dunara Castle" sailed on her maiden voyage in June 1875. Owned by Martin Orme & Co., who later amalgamated with John McCallum & Co. to form Mc-Callum, Orme & Co. Ltd., she sailed the Western Highlands and Islands. The "Dunara Castle" made frequent trips to St. Kilda and during the final evacuation she took the sheep, cattle, tourists and the last mail from St. Kilda to Oban on the 28th of August, 1930. After seventy three years of service she was finally laid up and scrapped in 1948.

Another regular visitor to St. Kilda was the S.S. "Hebrides", belonging to John McCallum & Co. This was a much more modern ship, being built in 1898. The S.S. "Hebrides" carried many hundreds of tourists to the island, including the last large group just prior to the evacuation in 1930. Twenty five years later the Hebrides was scrapped.

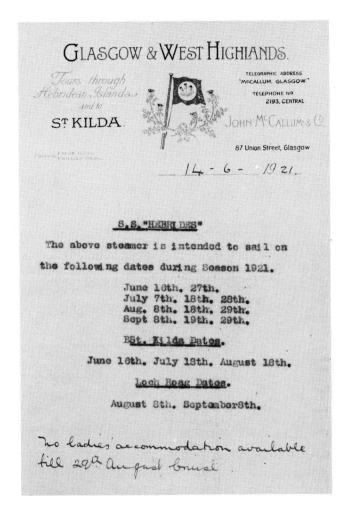

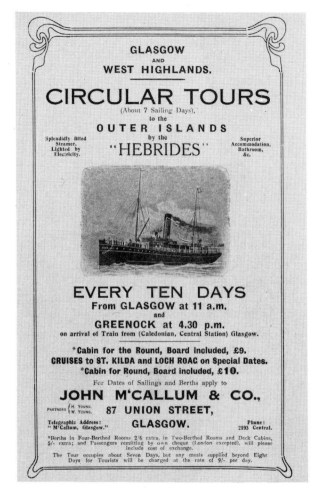

Only three sailings to St. Kilda were available on the S.S. "Hebrides" in 1921. With a two day sailing time, it was not always possible to fit the islands into a tour itinerary. Like today, advertising brochures were widely used and both shipping companies issued small pamphlets and guide books. John McCallum's guide, illustrated here, dates from 1912.

Visit the ROMANTIC
WESTERN·ISLES
and LONE S⸗ KILDA

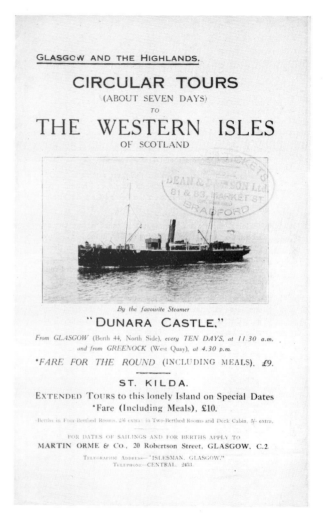

Costs for the tour were similar with either shipping line at £10 for the voyage to St. Kilda. The "Dunara
Castle" could carry about forty tourists on the Western Isles trip.

One of the natives is in the foreground taking stores to the village in this view while the "Dunara Castle" sits in the bay. This is one of a series of cards sold on board the ship.

Landing Stores at St. Kilda.

The concrete jetty in this view was built in 1901 at a cost of £600. While providing somewhere other than the shore to land visitors and provisions it was of little use to the steam ships. Rowing boats were still used to ferry passengers and goods to and from the island.

ANNUAL CRUISES TO ST. KILDA

St. Kilda Bay.

Main Street, St. Kilda.

St. Kilda Village.

ON SPECIAL DATES.

FARE FOR THE TRIP,
BOARD INCLUDED:

£10

Berths in Four-Berthed Room, 2/6 extra; in Two-Berthed Rooms and Deck Cabins, 5/- extra; and Passengers remitting by own Cheque (London excepted), will please include cost of exchange.

The Tour occupies about 7 days, but any meals supplied beyond 8 days to tourists will be charged at the rate of 9/- per day.

EARLY BOOKING ADVISABLE.

St. Kilda—Cliffs, 1,250 Feet High.

STEWARD'S RATES:

Breakfast,	...	...	...	3/-
Dinner,	...	...	...	4/-
Tea, ...	...	...	...	3/-

FIRST-CLASS CUISINE.

ST. KILDA VILLAGE.

An anonymously issued 1920's postcard of Village Bay. In fact, the photograph was taken in 1886 by Norman MacLeod for George Washington Wilson of Aberdeen. The curve of the street can be seen running from centre foreground. To the left is the round wall of the graveyard. Down by the shore are the store shed, manse and church.

Village Bay, St. Kilda, with whaling fleet at anchor   Copyright.

The whaling fleet shelters in Village Bay before heading for the whaling station at West Loch Tarbert, Isle of Harris. These ships, with names such as "Southern Cross" and "Southern Star", were crewed mostly by Norwegians. This postcard was issued anonymously at the turn of the century.

Crew of Whaling-station, Bunamhuinneddor. (Copyright.)

After leaving St. Kilda the whalers dropped their cargo at the whaling station on Harris to be processed. On the left and in the foreground are the remains of whale skins. At the turn of the century whale products were sought after for a multitude of uses and little of the carcass was wasted. It is only in the last seventy years that many substitutes for whale products have been found and hunting of them has declined.

Puffins, gannets, and fulmar inhabit the cliffs of the islands of the St. Kilda group. Their presence enabled the people to exist. In fact, these sea birds were essential to human life.

Donald Mc. Queen, fowling — Puffin Caught.

Snaring rods were used to catch fulmars and puffins, horse hair being imported from the mainland to be used in the manufacture of the nooses.

The flesh of these birds was actually boiled for eating. The eggs of the gannet were collected. No part of a bird was wasted.

FULMAR HARVEST ST. KILDA

The feathers of the fulmar were used for stuffing pillows, and the fulmar oil provided heat and light or was sold for use in medicines.

POST OFFICE. ST. KILDA

ST. KILDA VILLAGE

ST. KILDA SCHOOL, CHILDREN

ST. KILDA.

ST. KILDA PARLIAMENT

Posted in 1914, the message on this postcard reads "This is the whole population of St. Kilda, a place where I have been. Hardly any can speak English. I will be able to spin some yarns when I come home again ..."

ST. KILDA BAY

BOWERAY

FISHING, ST. KILDA

ST. KILDA.

LEAVING ST. KILDA

This multi-view card shows some of the various activities undertaken on the island as well as Boreray, another island in the St. Kilda group. The bottom right picture shows a small group of tourists leaving the island to return to their cruise ship.

St. Kildians with the famous Soa Sheep.   Copyright.

Soay sheep were a native breed to the St. Kilda island group. They were scrawny, wild and primitive in comparison to sheep on the mainland, and other islands. The card shows two native islanders with examples of the breed.

Soa, Wild Lamb, St. Kilda.

Tweed was manufactured from the wool of the Soay sheep and provided the St. Kildans with one of their few sources of income. A close-up of one of the Soay lambs, this postcard is probably a publicity photo for St. Kilda Tweed. In the background there are many bales of tweed and a notice proclaims the sheep to be a Soa (sic) Lamb.

These small rowing boats not only provided the St. Kildans with their only access to the outside world, but were also used for fishing and for travelling to other islands in the St. Kilda group. They were, therefore, important to the islanders and needed to be kept in good order. Most of the male population is seen in this view repairing one of the clinker-built boats.

Packing the Famous St. Kilda Tweed, St. Kilda

A large amount of the tweed produced on the island was sold to the many summer visitors. In 1911 some 3000 yards of tweed were produced with a retail value of £450 and by the end of the First World War, the entire production was sold to tourists aboard the "Hebrides" and the "Dunara Castle". In this view some of the islanders are packing the bales of tweed ready to be sold or shipped to the mainland on one of the tour ships.

Photographed outside the Factor's House, the male population and the children of St. Kilda sit. The Reverend Angus Fiddes sits on the right in the photograph. The minister was also employed on a salary of £5 per annum as sub-postmaster and worked from the Factor's House. The Post Box can be seen behind the Rev. Fiddes. Replaced in 1903 by a missionary by the name of Lachlan MacLean, Rev. Fiddes then left the island. The original Post Office was authorised in September 1899, opening for business in June 1900.

Members of St. Kilda Parliament

The St. Kilda Parliament were photographed in 1886 in the Main Street of the village. The Parliament sat every morning and decided the day's work. This view clearly shows two of the original thatched Black Houses, a frequent sight in most of the Western Isles. The day's work would involve a mixture of checking the sheep, milking the cattle, fishing and catching birds. This work was necessary, not only for food, but also to provide rent to pay MacLeod of MacLeod, the owner of the islands. This rent was mostly paid in kind, usually feathers, wool, tweed or bird oil.

Post Office, St. Kilda

The corrugated iron hut which served as the post office in later years was opened in 1913. Neil Ferguson, the Factor's representative, operated the Post Office from December 1906 to the final day in August 1930, often with the help of visiting tourists. Neil, the only native ·St. Kildan to act as Post-master, can be seen in this view published in 1929.

One of the few postally used cards from an Islander in my collection, the message reads: "Dear Mr. Milne, yours to hand few days ago and glad to hear you are all well as this leaves us all at present. Wee Mary was so pleased to get the sweets, did not get spoiled. If you go to Canada let me know. Wee Mary cried when I told her and if you go there be sure and write me from there, and may God be with you.

We have had an awful nice missionary this year, Mr. McLean, a very able speaker. Be sure and write me in no time. I am in a hurry just now. Your loving friend, William McDonald."

William McDonald lived in Cottage No. 3, Village Street and married Mary Ann McQueen in 1895. They had eleven children, including 'Wee Mary' and in 1924 the whole family left the island. R.M.R. Milne had been on St. Kilda the year before staying at the Manse.

Wreck of Wireless House by German Submarine, St. Kilda.

In May, 1918 St. Kilda became involved in the war against the Germans. A German submarine surfaced and the Captain issued a warning that he was going to attack the Wireless House. Over seventy shells hit the island, killing one sheep, frightening the residents and destroying the Wireless Station. Opened in the summer of 1913 using funds donated by the Daily Mirror and store magnate Gordon Selfridge, the Wireless Station was operated initially by Mr. Figuardo, a young Portugese gentleman, who instructed the Tiree-born missionary to St. Kilda, Mr. MacArthur, in its use. Rarely serviceable because of breakdowns and lack of funds, the Wireless Station was taken over by the Royal Navy in 1914, and abandoned in 1919.

Native St. Kilda.

Sixty-one year old Malcolm MacDonald appears in this still shot for the 1923 film 'St. Kilda; Britain's Loneliest Isle'. Malcolm lived in Cottage No. 8 on the island and died just before the evacuation. He lost his sight after the film, produced by Topical Productions of Glasgow, was made and was known as 'Old Blind Callum'.

Group of St. Kilda Women.

The married women in the community can be identified by the white headbands or 'mutches' as worn by the second and fifth women from the left on this postcard. They may be having a 'sit-down' but they were rarely idle, usually knitting socks and gloves.

The Village. Islanders, St. Kilda.

The village and islanders in 1884. Situated around Village Bay, the houses were built of stone with zinc roofs standing alongside the earlier thatched Black Houses. There were sixteen houses in all in a semi-circular formation along the street. A granite stone wall in front of the houses separated them from the cultivated strips.

Burial Ground, St. Kilda

For obvious reasons, not many tourists would send this scarce view of the little grave-yard on St. Kilda to their family and friends. Photographed in the 1880's it was to be the last resting place of many of the islanders before 1930.

The Manse, St. Kilda.

The Manse was built in 1830 and was followed by a building programme which resulted in the construction of some thirty new houses known as the 'New Village'. In the late 1890's a schoolroom was added to the existing church alongside the Manse.

In the Street, St. Kilda

The street was about twelve feet wide and constructed of slabs of granite. On the wall which separated the Village from the cultivated land an islander sits. Crops consisted mainly of barley and oats. Some vegetables were also grown.

Group of St. Kilda School Children

This 1886 picture by Norman MacLeod shows school master George Murray with fifteen of his pupils. Murray was a graduate of Aberdeen University and was contracted by the Ladies Association of the Highland Society to spend twelve months on the island as teacher during 1886-7.

Islanders with Nurse, St. Kilda.

This 1884 photograph, produced as a postcard in the early 1900's, was taken by Whyte of Inverness and shows the islanders with two new arrivals. On the extreme left is Mr. Campbell, the first school master sponsored by the Ladies Association of the Highland Society, while seated in the centre is Ann McKinley who, for a period of three years, was resident nurse on the island.

FAIRY CAVE, St KILDA.

D.A.M.

The 'House of the Fairies' or 'Fairy Cave' was a popular site with archaeologists and visitors. Finds in the 1840's included pottery and stone artifacts, some of which are now in the Royal Scottish Museum in Edinburgh. It was a pre-historic earth house and is described fully in the publication 'Buildings of St. Kilda'.

A St. Kildan woman shows four tourists her trade of spinning in the last years of occupation while another islander looks on. The women would pluck wool from the Soay sheep and work it to produce tweed for the tourists who visited.

ST. KILDANS SPINNING AND WEAVING

This card shows, from left to right: Neil Gillies, Donald Ferguson and Mary Gillies. Taken some time in 1935 at an exhibition in the UK the St. Kildans are demonstrating the production of tweed from wool to the finished product. Summer visitors still came to St. Kilda in the years after the Evacuation and Neil Gillies was there to welcome them. He sold postcards to them and the vast majority of these cards were stamped with a special cachet postmark. They were often posted at the next port of call, generally two days after leaving St. Kilda.

Village, St. Kilda

The final days came in 1930 when a petition to the Secretary of State for Scotland, signed by twelve men on behalf of the remaining population, was accepted. Plans for evacuation to the mainland were made and on the 28th of August, 1930 the last islanders, numbering less than forty, left St. Kilda.

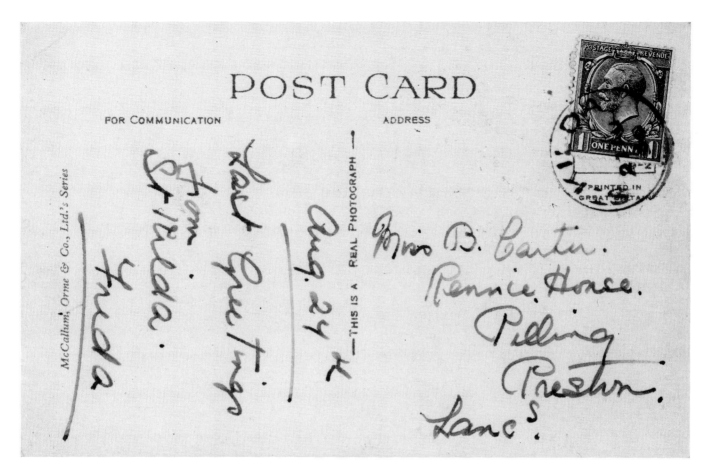

POST CARD

FOR COMMUNICATION   ADDRESS

McCallum, Orme & Co., Ltd.'s Series

THIS IS A REAL PHOTOGRAPH

Aug. 24

Best Greetings
from
St Kilda.
Freda

Miss B. Carter.
Rennie House.
Pilling
Preston.
Lancs.

This card was posted on the last day that the Post Office, second on the left in the postcard view (opposite), was in operation. St. Kilda's Post Office had its busiest day ever, although Neil Ferguson was too busy to run it. Instead, Alisdair Alpin MacGregor, author of 'A Last Voyage to St. Kilda' operated the Post Office, selling over 200 postcards and running out of 1d stamps by the end of the day! He did complain about the tourists, who were mainly from Lancashire, buying their stamps and postcards one at a time.

A SELECT BIBLIOGRAPHY

Buchanan, Margaret — St. Kilda—A Photographic Album, Blackwood, 1983.

Kearton, Richard & Cherry — With Nature and a Camera, Cassell & Co., 1897.

MacGregor, Alasdair Alpin — A Last Voyage to St. Kilda, Cassell & Co., 1931.

MacKay, James A. — Harris and St. Kilda, Islands Postal History Series: No. 1, Privately Printed, 1978.

MacLean, Charles — Island at the Edge of the World, Taplinger Pub. Co. Inc. (USA), 1980.

National Trust for Scotland — A St. Kilda Handbook, 1979.

Quine, David A. — St. Kilda Revisited, Dowland Press, 1982.

Royal Commission on the Ancient and Historical Monuments of Scotland — Buildings of St. Kilda, Royal Commission, 1988.

Steel, Tom — The Life and Death of St. Kilda, Fontana/Collins, 1975.

Williamson, Kenneth & Boyd, J. Morton — St. Kilda Summer, Hutchison, 1980.